Contents

Acknowledgements

A number of people have contributed to this booklet including those involved in the Taking Care of Education project, which is financially supported by the Gatsby Charitable Foundation: Louise Davies, Corporate Parenting Project Development Officer, Portsmouth City Council; Gerry Dermody, Project Director, Harrow Gatsby Project; and Pauline Inwood, Principal Officer, Education of Children Looked After, Derby City Council.

Also many thanks are due to those from Derby, Harrow and Portsmouth city councils who kindly commented on the drafts of the booklet.

Others who have contributed ideas and resources include: Helen Chambers, Principal Officer, Healthy Care Programme, National Children's Bureau; Jonathan Stanley, National Centre for Excellence in Residential Child Care, National Children's Bureau; and Mary Ryan, Independent Consultant, who wrote this booklet.

Particular thanks are due to Post Adoption Central Support (PACS), a voluntary organisation based in Scotland, for providing the inspiration for this booklet.

Who this booklet is for

This booklet is for teachers, teaching assistants, lecturers, school nurses, education support staff for looked after and vulnerable children, foster and other carers, residential child care workers, and parents of children and young people. This booklet seeks to:

- help teachers and others in education settings recognise attachment difficulties and consider how to help a child or young person achieve their full potential
- help parents, carers and others with care responsibilities recognise attachment needs and to work together with schools to support the child or young person's successful learning.

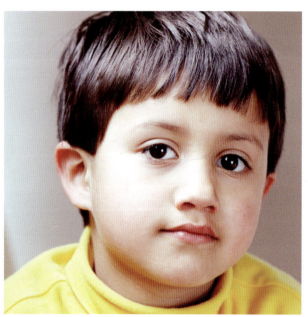

What it is about

This booklet describes behaviours and feelings that are common among many children and young people who have experienced a major loss or trauma early in their lives – these are known as 'attachment difficulties'.

Attachment difficulties can affect:

- anyone who has experienced a major loss and/or change in their life – for example, a child may lose the family around them when parents separate
- anyone who felt that their care was inconsistent or that they were neglected
- new families and others who care for vulnerable children – they need support and training to help them cope effectively with the effects of attachment difficulties
- teachers and other education staff who may have children in a class who have attachment difficulties.

It is important to remember that not all looked after children have attachment difficulties and not all children with attachment difficulties are looked after by a local authority.

The Taking Care of Education project was set up to support a small number of local authorities in order to bring together knowledge, resources and ways of working that might improve educational opportunities and outcomes for children and young people looked after by local authorities. Over the last six years the lead officers involved in the project have identified attachment difficulties as one of the challenges to accessing education that children and young people, and especially looked after children, can face. This booklet has been developed to increase knowledge and awareness of the need to support children and young people who have attachment difficulties.

The Healthy Care Programme, run by the National Children's Bureau and funded by the Department for Education and Skills, is a practical means of improving the health and well-being of looked after children and young people in line with the Department of Health Guidance *Promoting the Health of Looked After Children* (2002) and the Change for Children Programme. Find out more at: *www.ncb.org.uk/healthycare* and *www.everychildmatters.gov.uk/healthycare*

The National Centre for Excellence in Residential Child Care, based at the National Children's Bureau and funded by the Department for Education and Skills, is a collaborative initiative to improve standards of practice and improve outcomes for children and young people in residential child care in England. Find out more at: *www.ncb.org.uk/ncercc*

What are attachment needs and difficulties?

Babies and children need a secure emotional relationship with a main caregiver, usually a mother or father, in order to grow and develop physically, emotionally and intellectually. Babies and children need to feel safe, protected and nurtured by their caregivers so that they can gradually make sense of the world around them. This secure relationship with a main caregiver is essential for the child's development.

Sometimes this early relationship is missing, absent or broken for periods of time, perhaps because:

- there is a traumatic event that affects a child's continuity of experience
- the caregiver cannot meet the child's needs, for whatever reason.

The baby or child's attachment needs are not met, which leads to difficulties socially, behaviourally or emotionally, and these difficulties may impact on the child's learning and development. These are called attachment difficulties.

Looked after or adopted children and young people, including children who are unaccompanied asylum seekers, have often experienced emotional and physical neglect, physical and/or sexual abuse, poor parenting, family breakdown and, most importantly, separation from their main caregiver. Attachment difficulties can happen even if the child is living with the carer when the care is not good enough and the carer is not meeting the needs of the child. For some children, this may start at birth, or soon after, and for others it occurs repeatedly throughout their childhood years – for example, where a parent has mental health problems and is unavailable to effectively parent the child for periods of time. This separation affects the child profoundly and, for some children, affects their emotions, thoughts, identity and behaviour throughout their childhood even once they are in a secure and happy, permanent home, whether adopted or fostered.

A secure home environment, responsive carers and a stable experience of school are crucial factors in children's healthy physical and emotional development. When children become looked after, they may experience several changes of home and school, which adds to the lack of continuity and uncertainty that they may already have experienced. For example, they may be placed with foster carers, return to their birth family to try again, but have to return to different foster carers or a residential children's home if the relationship with their birth family breaks down. Children may then be moved to a more permanent placement. Some children may be placed in a different neighbourhood or local authority, or even a different part of the country. All these changes can lead to the child experiencing more separations that are stressful, confusing and unsettling; the child does not have a secure relationship with one main caregiver or a stable place to call 'home'. For some children and young people, school may be the one place that is constant and consistent.

'If you are in care you don't know what will happen to you. When I was told I was to live with a foster family, I worried too much and couldn't eat. I just went to despair.'

'Being in care is very difficult. There are lots of distractions about and I found I couldn't concentrate on my work.'

Change and circumstances affect everyone differently. Every child and family is unique and there is no one set of emotions, thoughts and behaviours that describes every child's experience of attachment difficulties; each child will adapt differently to their experience of loss and abandonment. However, there is a substantial body of information available to support schools, parents and carers who care for children who have had specific experiences. Resources listed at the end of this booklet provide more information on what is known about attachment difficulties and how to help children and young people.

How a child might feel and behave

A child who has experienced inconsistency, neglect, or loss of their main caregiver may suffer acute physical and emotional distress. Some commentators describe this as a 'traumatic injury'. Behaviour vividly describes feelings and offers insight into how a child has learned to cope with and survive loss. Every behaviour is a communication.

The following section about the effects on children of traumatic injury is drawn from Kate Cairns and Chris Stanway's work: *Learn the Child. Helping looked after children to learn*. It is believed that a child who has a traumactic injury may be affected in a number of ways, with some children more affected than others. Every child's experience and response is unique. It is known that attachment difficulties can affect physical and psychological functioning, and can be associated with other assessed needs, for example, ADHD and Dyspraxia.

Physiological effects

The child may be constantly aware of his or her surroundings – touch and smell may be as powerful as sight and sound and may instantly trigger memories or feelings of panic and fear. It may happen so quickly that he or she has no control over these feelings. To the child's teachers or carers, it may seem the child is suddenly misbehaving or has become withdrawn for no reason.

Hypervigilant: the child may always be looking around them, even behind them, to check what is happening. The child may have learnt to be constantly alert for possible danger so it is very hard for them to concentrate. He or she may be so busy listening and looking out for danger that he or she may not see or hear the everyday. The child may not hear the teacher's instructions because he or she anticipates a 'danger' message, not a normal message.

The child may have altered sleep patterns or eating patterns, he or she may self harm or be more prone to misusing substances such as alcohol or other drugs to escape from their feelings. The child may also try to avoid stressful situations, which may lead to avoidance of many everyday events and social interactions. School attendance may suffer. The child may not be able to distinguish what might be stressful or give an explanation for, or realise, why he or she may be acting in a certain way.

Physical effects

The child may experience physical and emotional problems such as:

- headaches
- digestive disorders
- respiratory disorders
- psychosomatic illnesses, such as, panic attacks
- muscle tension
- aching joints
- clumsiness
- altered spatial awareness.

Emotional effects

The child may not have developed, or may have lost, the ability to use reasoned thought and language to understand and explain behaviour; he or she may not be able to tell you why he or she is feeling or behaving in a particular way. It may be that he or she experienced the loss of his or her caregiver before he or she was able to speak or during the years language develops. It may be very hard for the child to describe his or her feelings because they are so painful.

Sometimes the child may find it hard to, or cannot, empathise with others – he or she may not understand how someone else is feeling.

The child may be extremely sensitive to others who have experienced stress and may be very aware of someone who is upset.

The child may only have a limited range of emotions, such as, terror or rage, with very little else. Sometimes the child's emotions may be unpredictable and friendships are difficult as other children find this frightening.

The child may not have, or may have lost, the capacity to experience curiosity and joy, and this may seriously impact on learning. The child may not be engaged or enthused by learning, he or she sees no fun in it, curiosity is not stimulated and there is no excitement about mastering skills or understanding.

Love, hope and gratitude may be unknown or uncommon in his or her life and, therefore, he or she may not know how to experience these emotions. Reciprocation or mutuality of anything good may be asking too much.

The child may not be able to take the risks necessary to learn anything new. He or she may have little self-esteem and may not be able to move beyond the comfort of the familiar.

The child who has experienced the terror, pain and isolation of abandonment may conclude that he or she is worthless, not 'wanted,' or maybe does not seem to exist at all, and with this comes great shame and loss of self-esteem. The child may desperately want to please, may never ask for help in case they look 'stupid', or, be the child who always wants the teacher to check their work. He or she may hate making mistakes and may not be able to bear criticism. He or she may seek popularity with other children at any cost; the child may do anything his or her peers ask, or may be very expert at telling adults what they want to hear.

The child may be withdrawn or defiant. It may be hard for those close to him or her to see defiance as a sign of hope, a sign that the child is struggling to hold on to esteem and identity.

The child might have suffered extreme abuse and he or she may take on some aspects of the identity of their abuser and may, for example, harm themselves or others. Or, he or she may take on another identity such as 'a caretaker' who acts as a protector.

Every child reacts differently to unmet attachment needs and there is no one set of behaviours to describe every child's difficulties.

Social effects

The child may have learnt early in life that he or she must choose the safer option and may have to make a choice within a few seconds without time to consider other options. The child may jump up as soon as a door opens, or refuse to do an activity unless he or she can do it their way or with a certain group of friends. This may also lead to the child limiting what he or she will do because he or she must always choose what he or she knows to be safe.

The child may have diminished impulse control and may find it difficult to make and keep friends, which may lead to him or her being solitary or lonely. The child may end up mixing with peers who accept or even promote unpredictable and anti-social behaviour. The child may not be able to empathise with others and so cannot understand and learn from them, and this may affect the child's ability to make and maintain relationships.

The child may frighten others with their extreme reactions of terror or rage, which may lead to the child feeling more afraid and socially isolated.

It may be hard for the child who is always alert to possible danger to concentrate on the everyday business of getting on with others. This may not be a priority for him or her, so he or she does not benefit from being sociable.

It may be difficult for the child to maintain friendships because he or she cannot use language to explain his or her behaviour. Other children may find this odd and unsettling. This may lead to the child experiencing further isolation and rejection, and consequently fewer opportunities to learn from relationships.

Every day, the child with attachment difficulties may be dealing with thoughts and feelings of:

- loss
- control
- rage
- helplessness
- pleasing others
- rejection or abandonment
- identity.

How a child might behave and why

Why is ...	Maybe because ...
Katie constantly turning around in class?	Danger often comes from behind.
Jodie often ignoring the teachers' instructions?	Jodie is so alert to everything around her that she cannot hear the teacher's instructions.
Jamal always exploding during maths or spelling?	Jamal finds it difficult to be wrong or make mistakes, and it is always obvious when answers in maths or spelling are wrong.
Rebecca not wanting to go to school?	The exams are about to start and Rebecca is very worried about failing or not doing well.
Kelly in trouble at playtime or during moves between classrooms?	Kelly feels more secure in small groups – preferably with people she knows. She feels panicky in crowds.
Wesley refusing to be helped with new work?	Wesley wants certainty in his life and never wants to feel helpless again, so he finds it very hard to accept any help.
Harrison often taking other pupils' belongings?	Stealing is often linked to early loss, especially of caregivers, and this can lead to a more general misunderstanding of the difference between 'mine' and 'yours'. Harrison had little of his own in his early life.
Sarah constantly asking the teacher trivial questions about her work?	Sarah has very low self-esteem and needs to feel an adult is close to her constantly. She may feel she cannot bear to get it 'wrong' or the teacher may 'disappear' like others have in her life, for which she blames herself.
Ben's behaviour suddenly getting much worse?	Something has happened that is hard for him to cope with. Perhaps a new sibling has arrived, or there is a painful anniversary, or a visit to his birth family, or changes at home. Stress can be in the past, now or in the future.
Adam being sulky and refusing to speak with the teacher or others in authority about difficulties?	Adam has no words to describe how he feels, so, looking sulky is a communication.
Merline frequently telling lies?	Telling lies is often linked to early loss, especially of caregivers, and leaves children with difficulties distinguishing between fact and fantasy. Merline's early life had no boundaries and she has difficulty describing her feelings. She is also desperate to be liked and will say what she thinks will please.
Charlie sometimes very quiet and withdrawn; he often seems to be in a world of his own?	Charlie finds it safer not to respond to or engage with others, especially adults, when he finds a situation stressful.

Case study 1: Michael

Background

Michael is 13 years old and in Year 9 at secondary school. His behaviour has improved significantly since he first joined the school and he now does reasonably well and has made good friends within his class. Michael is living with foster carers and their two younger children and it is expected he will live with them until he leaves care. Michael was in and out of care frequently during his childhood as his parents struggled to care for him. Michael has regular contact with his father but no contact with his mother.

Michael describes what happened

'I saw my Dad at the weekend – I only see him about every month, usually at his place or sometimes we go out. I like to see him because he is my Dad. When I went to his flat on Saturday we watched a new video and had a takeaway but then he told me that my Mum has a new boyfriend and she's going to have a baby. I couldn't really understand because I haven't seen my Mum for about two years and then she was still doing drugs. I wanted to cry but I couldn't. All week, I kept getting into trouble at school, I just wanted to smash something – how come she can have another baby but not want me?'

Michael's teacher wonders, why?

'Michael is usually a reasonable pupil but suddenly his work has deteriorated and I am getting reports of angry and rude behaviour from his subject teachers. He has been asked to leave the classroom and see the head of year on several occasions this week. I asked him if there was a problem but he became very sulky and refused to say anything. I am at a bit of a loss about what to do. This is so sudden. The next step is to put him on report.'

Relevance of attachment issues

Contact visits with birth parents and families are sometimes painful for looked after children. Parents and children may desperately want to remain in contact even though it raises mixed feelings. Children and young people may be reminded that their parents cannot care for them and feel angry and sad about this but have nowhere to direct these feelings. It may also reawaken their feelings of loss and abandonment. It can be hard for children and young people to contain such strong feelings, which they may spill out into other parts of their life. It is also very difficult for them to talk about their feelings – they may not have the words to explain, or they may feel ashamed of their feelings.

Case study 2: Naomi

Background

Naomi is seven years old and in Year 3 of primary school. This is her second primary school and she has been living with foster carers for the last 18 months. It is unlikely that Naomi will return to her birth family. She has a younger sister whom she sees every three months.

Naomi describes what happened

'My teacher is very nice and I like her very much. I like school a lot and I have lots of friends now. My teacher said we were going to do a new project called 'all about me' and we have to bring pictures of ourselves as babies to put on the wall and ask our mums and dads to tell us stories about what we were like when we were little. I felt very scared when she told us about this because I don't see my mum like everyone else and I don't have any pictures of me as a baby. My mum didn't want me or my sister. My friends don't know that I live with a different mum and dad.'

Naomi's teacher wonders, why?

'Naomi is usually very keen to do everything I ask and always has good attendance and meets all her targets. Recently she has been off school quite a lot – tummy aches etc. but nothing specific – and is constantly asking to go to the toilet during group work activities. I am wondering if she is being bullied or doesn't get on with someone in her group. Her work is suffering, too.'

Relevance of attachment issues

It is very common for looked after and adopted children to have no photos or stories to tell about their early childhood. In fact, they may have very sad memories that they would not wish to share with school friends. Children can feel exposed, ashamed and 'different' by activities such as these. They may not have told friends that they are adopted or looked after, and are likely to have very mixed feelings about their birth parents. They may not want to talk to carers or adoptive parents about this, fearing this may upset the carers or parents, too.

Case study 3: Sammie

Background

Sammie is 10 years old and in Year 5 at primary school. She has been in this school for a year and lives with foster carers and their family. She seems to be happy and settling well although she is a very anxious child and needs to have her friendship group around her to feel secure.

Sammie explains what often happens

'I don't like lunch times because we all have to go in the playground and there are too many people rushing round and the little ones are making noise. Then, each class has to line up when we are told to go to the hall for lunch. At lunch you have to choose what you want and I don't always like it and sometimes I can't sit with my friends. I am always getting told off for not eating my dinner because I'm talking. Sometimes I feel hungry in the afternoons and I get grumpy. I like mornings best at school, really.'

Sammie's teacher wonders, why?

'Sammie is like a changed person in the afternoons; she can't settle down to anything properly and is always talking to others on her table, distracting them. Sometimes I have had to put her on her own which she really doesn't like. I don't think she eats her lunch and have asked the dinner ladies, who say she doesn't eat much. I don't really know what to do as we can't force her to eat.'

Relevance of attachment issues

Many children with attachment difficulties find large groups quite threatening. They become hypervigilent and constantly scan the environment for danger. They are not likely to be aware they are doing this, as it is an automatic response to being in a stressful situation. Some children will also be very dependent on their friendship group and only feel safe when they are with their friends – they will often go to great lengths to be with their friends, because they are the safer option.

Food and eating can be very difficult for some children and young people and, in a stressful situation, they may lose their appetite or overeat for comfort. They may not be able to settle long enough to eat a meal (meals may have previously been erratic or something to eat quickly) or they may crave food that gives a quick burst of energy.

Case study 4: Marcus

The scene

Marcus is 15 years old and in Year 10 at school. He has been at this school for three years and so far is only just meeting his targets. His teachers constantly say that he does not work even though they believe he is able. They believe he can achieve academically, if he puts in the work and effort. He is also known for having a volatile temper and is frequently sent out of class following an outburst, often about uncompleted work. Because Marcus has become taller and bigger, some teachers find his behaviour threatening. Marcus lives in a residential children's home and has been back and forth between different carers and his birth mother many times. He is determined to keep in contact with his birth mother and still sees her occasionally, but has come to accept that he cannot live with her.

Marcus explains what often happens

'I don't see the point of all this work at school. Even when I do what they want, they are still going on at me, I could have done this or written a bit more. What's the point of me doing it if it's still not good enough? Some teachers are ok but some just needle me all the time – like they don't think much of me – they say stuff like, "No homework again, Marcus? It'll hardly be worth you sitting the GCSE, will it?". If I'm having a bad day, I just explode when they say something like that and get chucked out of the classroom, but at least I don't have to listen to them getting at me.'

Marcus's teacher wonders, why?

'Marcus has always been a difficult pupil and we try to give him some extra space, but it is frustrating when it is clear he hasn't even tried to do the work or has done the bare minimum – it is like he can't be bothered. In class discussions or group work he often does really well but somehow he just can't get it written down. We have tested for dyslexia, so it's not that. Some of his subject teachers seem to particularly set him off and, this year, we have seen a lot more of his temper – shouting at teachers, slamming books on the desk – not actually physically threatening someone, but definitely causing a disruption in the classroom. Marcus is now spending more time sitting in the library instead of being with his class and we can't allow this to continue; we have to do something.'

Relevance of attachment issues

Children and young people with attachment issues may fear failure and so will not put themselves in a position where they might fail. School work is, by its nature, commented on along with suggestions for improvement and these children may interpret this as failure. These are the children who often do not work at school even though their teachers say they are able pupils. For them, rejection has been a common experience throughout their lives and they will not want to risk feeling that again – in any part of their life. For some children, being told off in school or receiving sarcastic comments can reawaken the intense feelings of distress following repeated rejections by their main caregiver, and some children and young people cope with this through angry behaviour.

So how can I help you to understand?

There are many ways in which you can help me with my attachment needs and difficulties but they will be different for other children and their situations.

It is harder for me if you only focus on problems and what I can't do.

Here are some ideas that have worked.

How you can help me:

- Understand that I have strengths and sometimes you focus too much on what I can't do rather than what I can do.

- Talk to each other - my parents, carers, social worker and other staff at school - to help you understand me better and find out what I do well and what I find difficult.

- Make a plan with me to help me through the day or difficult times - it could be about what I like and what I need to avoid, or times of the day like getting up, meal times and bedtimes, or how to help me when I am upset or angry.

- Tell me when I am managing my behaviour well - I need to know when I have improved. Telling me 'well done' because I didn't yell at someone when they annoyed me or, I asked before borrowing someone's pen does help me.

- Help me to recognise my feelings. It helps if you name it and tell me how I am looking and may be feeling. 'You're looking happy, smiling and relaxed.' 'You're looking puzzled and screwing your eyes up, is something worrying you?' If I can talk about it I will, but respect my feelings if I can't.

- Tell me in advance about any changes, such as new teachers or going on visits - I need a little bit of time to get used to new things and people and it helps to be reminded about what happens next, such as lunch is in 10 minutes. I feel safer if I know what to expect.

- **I may find it hard to remember to have the right equipment on the right days, such as PE kit, so making sure my parents or carers know will help me.**

- Sometimes I need to be on my own to calm down - can we agree on a safe place for me to go and a quick way for me to tell you I am going? I will only use this when I really need to.

- Sometimes I do feel angry and I don't know why - please let me know that's OK so long as I don't hurt myself or others.

- I might find it hard to look at you directly but it doesn't mean I am not listening to you - don't ask me to look at you if I find it difficult.

- Sometimes it is easier for me to draw or write a story about why something happened than to talk to you about it.

- My behaviour is telling you how I am feeling. It is important that you stick to the plans that we have made for helping me through these difficult times.

And most importantly:

- I do appreciate you being there for me and trying to understand me even on the days when things are difficult.